A Middle North

A Middle North

Poems

Robert Stark

LEAKY BOOT PRESS

A Middle North: Poems
by Robert Stark

First published in 2014 by
Leaky Boot Press
http://www.leakyboot.com

Copyright © 2014 Robert Stark
All rights reserved

No part of this book may be reproduced or
transmitted in any form or by any means,
electronic, mechanical, photocopying,
recording, or otherwise, without prior
written permission of the author.

ISBN: 978-1-909849-13-6

Acknowledgements

I am delighted to acknowledge the contrivance of several magazine editors & poets in the prior publication of some of these poems: *The Delinquent, The New Hampshire Review, Almost an Island: A New Anthology of Fife Writings, Le Zaporogue*. Muchos gracias amigos. Jim Goddard (most of all) made this collection happen, that is his habit, and minimized the shabbiness of its sentimentalism. Likewise, Seb Doubinsky owns my thanks for the wonderful translations of Baudelaire that do more than keep the ear in when I have been unable to write a scant line: hardening and firming what would otherwise be flabby, and for his invigorating haiku-like flashings.

For my nieces: Emma, Holly, Anya, & Bethany, I'm grateful and sorry for my continuing & prolonged absence.

Finally, for Malcolm X, Chelsea Manning, Julian Assange, Glenn Greenwald, Jeremy Scahill, Ed Snowden, and Cornell West. The inadequacy of this book is perhaps most obvious in this paragraph. Love to each of you, my teachers, and my brothers, & to Amy Goodman, without whom contemporary awareness would be impossible. And to Bobby Sands and to Frederick Douglass.

Thanks also to my students at Exeter University who chose to care.

Hang ups, let downs
Bad breaks, set backs
    —Marvin Gaye

For Lisa J. Trochmann
& for Tom Clayton

After a fashion

Pomes de Liban

Everything will depend on the hesitation
—Mallarmé

I

A day, a night
& the hour of departure lengthens
into this high perpetuity
of leaving   above weather
above human time nothing is less permanent
than a day   than a night.

How could we know what water bird
you were poised there
for all time   what kind
or species or whether you were even there
o haughty water bird, reckless of regard
by the Lake of the Isles   if you were there or no.

II

On their raised red brick home outside my home
two salamanders idle
in the morning & the midday sun:
all day   but when I look they steal away.

I scarcely see & cannot not imagine them:
so arch an image
of dragon & how proud a second
in the corner of my eye   then shy.

Could I live in fire as they
I would not be so chaste, not darting coy
as they: a Triton flashing on the land
could I live in fire   could I live in fire.

III

As though I had rolled a tiny petal
in my hand, so lingers the scent;
& as fragrance may not spill at once
from such a flower, so your letters are

never late, or unexpected:
of night Jasmin, it may be,
a name I thought I overheard
in the Palm Garden with the whores last night,

the same *white-flower-o-the-Jasomine*
I called you once having half-remembered
another's song, another's dream
(I overheard my love, I merely overheard).

IV

The springtime branch I bore for you, away
from the parent olive tree has dried now
& it abides my acquisitiveness with equanimity:
its parched secrets scorn to break up in my hand.

What oak leaf, in what book of myths might say
more on longevity? & stubborn
as an insect in its skin of bone
is the ruin of intent

fragile & jealous, loveliness
is always what it might have been
what it was before the awful gesture
the taking anyhow.

V

The driver just took me aside: nor A nor B
as though for pomegranates was the only for
for thinking on or stopping at
between the road & home

(beading arils on a tiny pin
bitter gems & scant, for me
indifferent in my pride was there ever such a tree
as pomegranate?) About to reach for one

he doesn't, hesitates & brings a riper down
(his sons are grown now, men all three) cuts in:
& now the seed & pith, the enveloping succulence,
the whole story of the man.

VI

Talk to me no more, you say, of Karenina,
of the thrum of love & malice in the heart
so we turn back   & the lilacs are faded:
what barrenness

has eaten of the flower's heart?
The olive trees are washed
an unthinkable white & gray,
their tendrils' ancient roundelay is moribund

a fly beneath the swatter's hand:
what gossamer   what wing diaphanous?
We do not know but feel that it is so.
E'er since your speech rang true
            I've sounded it for dross.

Failaka

There was a moment
when it seemed we might have stayed:
another bus tour, that round
of crazygolf that had to wait

upon our camel driver
& his unsightly, ankle-bound
camel sow, bitten, fretted
in the wayward heat;

such staggering domesticity
we had to turn about
got into the minivan
& couldn't look, wide-eyed

great-humped tottering like
a sack spinning on a spike
the quite unenviable symbol
we had crossed a Gulf to see.

A tightness of the skin needs
to be acknowledged. It is true
we felt something natural
returning to the boat

our ordinary robinsonade
expiring only slowly as we watched
Tom & Jerry on repeat & waited
word of the storm.

At Byblos

> shut them in
>   With their triumphs and their glories and the rest
>   —Browning

For John & Mahboubeh

Off the map we walk
the newer Roman road & likely
between sarcophagi I say
I am perhaps in love
with you you laugh you scoff

& I cannot convince you
that history lies
beyond understanding,
that history is the love
that was & was not so.

The precarious
permanence of sandstone
for example: once heaved
into the nympheum,
the goddess' living form

is crumbled now to atoms
& derelict of all lies
in its authentic atmosphere.
Blank obelisks have lasted
longer—there

is always some bewildered
pious soul to prop them up,
some uncertain worshipper
out of abstract joy to deny
the wrecking gods an execration.

Was nymph limbed, ever, as these
strange rocks? The superstitious flock
here now with their cameras and drop
their cigarettes right into the bowels
of History—what is there to see

but the original perplexity
of matter & the certainty of being
just some other clutter
that will & will not last
like love. You laugh you scoff

but no one even knows
which god they worshipped here.

In Memory of Peter Firchow

You are young in my only photograph
in love & in a foreign country drawn
to that long unvisited familiar place
wherever it is, the traveller's skyey home

that world of well-made cars & mountain pass
-es that might as well have never been
being so far gone: ah the camera cheats
us into memory
     & if the students ask
you were a bug, you were a nightingale,
you were even dust when Hardy put to task
Shelley on the count of loss, a realist
in this if nothing else, vital
& sensitive & undeceived at last
that same traveller, that same, that high path.

For J. C.

I have your satchel on
the kitchen table
& I have ransacked your home
for medication

to no avail: what use
the alcoholic's bag?
his stash of sleeping pills
& supplements?

Not quite dead you sit alone
not noticing the strangers
around you
you are in their home now

& it is their game: you play
the fabled bird   ashen, waiting
waiting for the moment
for the right moment to take off

While Yet She Lives

For Sèbastien Doubinsky

My poet is not afraid of the dark
My poet bears darknesss
Lightly in her human heart

My poet compels your poet
To put down his weapon & desist
My poet revolts against his hypocrisy:

He is chastened. My poet must not
Ever or again be caught red-handed
Insisting that justice prevail in lawless lands.

My poet will not sit at your table.
My poet will sit on your table.
My poet furnishes her own table.

Sweet, bloodless, she contrives
upon my imagination like a fugue
long rehearsed: as tho', for her, reserve
were a scrutible fact. A

half-life not her own & yet somehow
the very bead of essence. Her triumph:
to find soul in the phantastikon of man
any man, in his drivelling infancy

thinking only of the moment &
perhaps, hoping, gasping
toward the next open mouth
an ecstatic forever.

The facts defy mythology
& I her lunatic brother am aghast
& anguished near her
3000 miles near her

long enough & far:
how is it that we lack humanity
finding our creatures, losing them
to go on?

A Sardonic

Early to market the hawker of flowers
it is a day laid by for love: pent up
too long in ice & hoar the humming waters
& pent too long on reft branch the chirrup
frail of our melodious native songsters:

Now is the lustrous yellow buttercup
close by & in anticipation glares
fierce upon the lover's neck & does keep
it there (for today is Valentine's Day)

Love's overgenerous imprint to mock,
the condominium squalor & the in
of it & lo the green world come back again
the racing world, & cruel of display:
thou hast chained hand to foot & bade me walk.

The Bilbao Effect

Have you been to Bilbao? Then shut up.
The Europeans understand, accept
the Architect, not your yankiedoodle
whatnot. The fact about art? It's a small
Italian town; you get lost quick. If

you're happy to be lost then great.
The struggle for *Beauty*, well crafted work,
the Bilbao Effect, well. Gehry didn't
think it any good. Architecture is
trying to understand the need

for shape without allegiance, sacrifice.
Be a good neighbour. Don't talk down
to the audience. *Curate. Curate. Curate.*
& then, nothing but that shotgun courthouse,
Post Office, library: no building neutral,
no neutral building: Thank you, Chicago.

This Marine Comes Home

For Mr Borox

He wears a slogan on his sleeve: *I Love
Boobies* & you can tell from this eagerness
to talk he is simpatico. Many
a hundred feet a man may fall or fly
into the impervious: the Terminal

fills with his compatriots: a different loudness,
not battle. Manners never more correct
than now, awash with *where do children learn
to cry*? An insincerity

arises with the first pert girl
I spot & confirms the hate I owe to these
White Samaritans—black babes almost at the breast
in the airport talking God, for whom
War is a series of motherable tragedies.

The Bard O' Cream Toon

George Washington decked out in ambergris,
a fallen sojer greaving on the floor,
Dr. King notoriously displaced: wedged
twixt storefronts, an excellent water-nymph
now in the public library & thee

Rabbie—*un*expected—far flung so from Ayr,
strange & tall: this city has a queer way
with statues: you've become a Grecian-eyed
traffic-warden. What is that you say? *Hmmmpph?*

The mouth I know! Your poet's brave backside
looks exposed now: a braw new condo's edged
all winter up behind you: much wrangling
with the workforce & there was picketing
about 'Burns Commons' & speechless irony.

Black times at Laacke, Joys & Co. so help us:
the galleria's closed, the picket line
itself is barely manned at Faith Incorp.
the grievance being so goddamn obvious
all agree who pass: there I met a man,
a small elusive man, well-known, who rounds
at closing time, the bars & sells strange wares
to drunks: sausages & pepperoni.

He sits a while & they come up to him
jesting a bit, hungry,
but if it pays I cannot tell. I found
him digging at the ice all winter long,
smiled each time & now the ice is gone
he digs there still; digs & sells
from bar to bar these sausages,
whatever it is they are.

He rakes around for things to eat
or else to pass the time. The seagulls cry
around him in the park & on the bridge,
the crooning gulls who have the best of it
now Old Milwaukee's bust. A sign proclaims
on Library Hill, on North Avenue,
Van Buren & St Paul—Hell, all the Saints
& the Bar Association agree

& the Realtors on the bus-shelters
rejoicingly—<u>YOU</u> CAN HAVE IT <u>ALL</u>—
& so this day-digging & this small-beer
capitalism provide a living
honest & well-meaning. He always has
an unassuming ruffle for the dog,
the scratch he knows,
best-loved behind the ear.

We smile & in greeting are sincere:
no interrogator, I am loath
to traipse the fen Wordsworthian
but—& *that's* perhaps the thing—no sadness
seems to come upon his face or onto mine,
no wisdom is left there unspoken, no rhyme
leaps: am I to blame that cannot see it
for this sheer broad-shouldered civility?

Does not some arrogance in my nature
need his loneliness for companionship?
Well, I wonder what he's digging at.
I wonder what it is he sells in bars to drunks.
I wonder, when I sit home & listen
as the neighbours fuck, about this man
whose desire & hurt are as my own,
what I am digging at, what selling.

May Street, March

Incongruence of generation mars
this town: were there means to crush the earth
when these houses were put up, squat
rectilinear roughly 2D man
-hattanesque confabulations would be ours

but the gables did not square
with the aboriginal geography
where chimneys vault in echelon, lead
gulls & pigeons nightly to the stoop,
a sort of landing strip, or signal fire

& a veritable warmth. Sfumata
of dusk & the red brick fades: life exudes
the interminable solitude of being
poised always at this window:
fingers know the keys, not which key.

Sixteen years away & nothing baffles
as that most harshly thrust aside:
tabloid & testosterone & highstreetism
I have no complaint
but a body's awkwardness in transiting

England; I have been content to watch
while some exquisitely busy young & perhaps
happy people idle on the cathedral lawn;

trees have been planted, grown & gone
in the time that this business has played out:

baptism & gossip & the privilege
of summer. Whatever it is
abundance call it, is not a fantasy
nor is it particularly rare. Frisbees
are surely the least monkish of miracles

for instance: levity eluded us
for centuries and now we toy with it,
throw it for the dog. Fly with it
amigo: if I could
catch it in my mouth I would.

Easter Sunday Breadline

For Jeremy Scahill

Sweat that seems to sigh, blood
through skin, shuddering limb
on limb, mind that speaks
tongues, screws aside:
on Al Jazeera I hear we live
on 'public bread';
it sells for four times less
than what it costs to make.
There is no wheat,
no money for the wheat;
few bakers, too few gardeners.

At Tunis & Tahrir
a sacrifice forgot;
in Virginia (sweet Virginia, O)
the *antic* sits & waits,
humiliations overcome
a naked soul in uniform
contemplates. How
the decrepit fourth estate
flinches now assassination
is the law, the self
-licking ice-cream-cone

of terror. To imagine
life rather than to live;
to lose a lover to the whim
of some salaried man,
an executive and a suave
well-spoken president; to be
collateral, unmentioned
in the statistics, dealt with
more or less approximately;
unmade in the sudden furious
burn of the authorized strike

once was inconceivable.
Nothing Dantescan here
no *contrapasso*, no purge
since the bomb & Vietnam;
imagination pales when
cluster bombs chew corpses,
when phosphorous thaws the bone,
when the magnanimity of the blast
fuses tragic friends.
Had Dante genius to devise
disposition matrices,

had he thought to keep souls there
without learning their names
or heeding of their stories
but rather marking how
such a one is of a given sex & age
was born in some-such place
of notorious parentage,
Hell were not wide enough;
that best edict of chaste form
& patterned grace must be
horrified & ghastly overfed.

The world is a rubbled battlefield
& pandemonium enough.
In the suburbs of the West

where rumor scarcely reaches—
threshold, limbo—
tributary highstreetism
ferries the complacent &
uncomprehending from
one vaguely awkward place
to another, almost discernibly
less comfortable place.

This is the penalty:
to neither go nor tarry;
the humdrum apocalypse
speaking a different language,
worshiping another god, failing
to disrupt the league tables
or castigate the boss;
safe within our palaces
of self we needn't know
how one surrenders to a drone,
or refutes unspecified misdeeds.

Morbid, is it, to scrutinize
the vector, to insist
on the arithmetic of hate,
the calculus of loss;
maudlin to be found
thus consumed & feverish,
knowing there is not enough
empathy to go around?
What of it? Today
the stiff lies in the street;
tomorrow we may bury it.

Note in Winter

Down, down
Now we have your yesterday:
A ten-year low.

Hopeless I
Crave word:
All right are you Leez?

Weeks ago, falling
Asleep I worried:
I worry.

A simple nod
Agreeable
Tacit endorsement

Ah, to allay . . .
Or send even
Blankness

But, Leez, you *are* ok?

'Love' (trans.)

It was a part of speech
which part I never knew
a thing to name a kitten
the embryonic thing

in the shirt pocket, the purr
of name become established
in the home, pouncing
guests. *Lublu* was a beast

to visitors, tore the screen door
one time when the plumber came
harassed our guests
but somehow loved us.

On the silver birches of
our outer-hands she slew
remembrances, they never bled
but lowped for days

temporary, written, red,
the siren to beware of, laying
love haphazardly in the creature
we would fondle on the couch

who irks to destroy & whose
inclination at a moving object,
part study part intent
is but to play until disinterest & death.

In Invalid Time

The spider's puce rent-worm spins in its cob:
Lacunae waxing in a rot of text.

A Riddle at the Land Fill

Among them, stifling her bright laugh,
she has the guts to ask the man
the name of the dog.

He gives her three guesses.
Spotty. He gives her a clue.
Sam. Josh. But the dog

is named *Jack*: he is lovely
jumping around like that
with the ball & the stick!

The tiger-coloured butterflies,
the milk-white smaller
& less graceful ones

twinge in the sunlit air;
in its frantic totemism
the creature doesn't see them.

Villanelle

There was no lesson, no meaning, in the rain,
But with phantom sensibility
It simply fell, dimly on the sleeping man

Who seemed to welcome it amid the mundane
Picaresques & vapour-reckonings of day;
There was no lesson, nor meaning in the rain

But a munificence he could not explain.
No longer conscious of the new calamity
That simply fell, dimly on the sleepy man

The restive insomnolent overthrown
Man who had read the note: *inclined . . . to marry*,
There was no lesson, no meaning, in the rain;

A feeble shrug of wakefulness obtained
Votive calm, but it did not satisfy, precisely:
It simply fell, dimly on the sleeping man;

In the obscure capital of Affection
The sky crashed in the street. Dawn was hours away.
There was no lesson, no meaning, in the rain.
It simply fell, dimly on the sleeping man.

As an eye mote tries
the range of sense & trues
so streams this

blown cottonwood by
coaxing us beyond ourselves.
We see precisely

what we must never focus on:
there's nothing here
of the gamboling butterfly

whose easy stunt is fellowed,
often, with a prancing friend;
together they are happy

happy, too, alone: we
should study them in this
their dance & in the silent music

that enshrouds & bids them on
o still cottonwood,
in your element, we follow

with what mind we can.

Dream Lay

In the recess of some other mind I
wake in the midst of it,
forever waking & forgetting it,
the nothing of my fantasy.

You might have banished me, perhaps you did:
less bashful, less wide-eyed
but at the end still the child that wanted you
to kiss him & was ashamed to feel so

keenly those foreign attentions: the curl
of your pronunciation at his ear,
humid, nearly adolescent palms &
the childish giggling not far off: friends.

Those provinces were warm & yet
a cosy alliance in History
was the most that I could summon then.
Yes, I appreciate the irony.

This morning I awoke from your arms,
this morning I nearly remembered,
this morning   but how could you know
being then a child & now
my brooding invention
I lay with you the whole time.

Gulfs

The water's island
speech has but a single thought
that to the shore is more

infinite than the totality of sand can ever be
to the mercurial
grain. The way it is

the clattering & draft
of pebble rears the thing
in talk   talk   talk

of which it is about:
forming formlessness,
the trepidation of bedrock

it gives new realm of course
to seaworms, pools
for algae (oxidized & warm)

the microcosm
of sand patterned like a Zen-garden,
the multifariousness (I

have looked for you incontinently)
of spiral-spired shells
discarded in unflinching lines,

universes each unto themselves
(I have been reminded)
to be discovered, named

above all, Time—the effluvium
Omar Khayyám smote
in two bare hemistiches—

imagine then you are (i.e. finally
in death) what heretofore you were:
not perishable but unremembering,

human & in-borne—to give to each
of us an artery,
unabrogated being,

the kierotic form
of our arid selves
in our own catastrophe

how necessary, then,
the rigid beachcombers
& their silhouettes that stoop pellucidly

to the idle, temporary pools
of the dusked tide: a truth they seek
that survives in being transformed.

The chagrined pooch that longs
for the tennis ball to be thrown again
& again: he also lends his voice,

a desperate, baffled, insufferable when
have we been more than this
dear, fanatic, wave-wombed friend?

There is no rush, can be
no rush in anything that gives & takes
forever (as though to gauge how far fallen from intent

is the surf that rises from the heart).
Whatever else we may say it isn't—
we are not—just tossed off to be done with

but sounded with deliberate voice,
brazen & obsessive, audible.
If we were to make the quotient

of our talk which is most urgent
to each other always our sole measure:
the difference, then.

So, yesterday's rain
Squeaking in the grass
A first abundance
A spring

That follows
What sense next
Must recollect
Or choose

Remembering
Whatever comes from the sky
(Or half remembering)
May lie

Longer in the earth
Than fact would have it
There, an impediment
A birth.

Imagine! In the sea
confiding 'til
arms elbows sculpted
palms unlearn
the ease of air

Deeper. Another
thrown moon
another vaulted
intractable sky
& light of verdigris

Thus I, Persephone
thus do I rapt descend
or rise unto your realm,
thus Love rises or descends
& dare it gasp?

     Queen of the Haugh
    Suspended in a clearing
      That afternoon,
      Was it evening?
That summer when the heat was all
    Across Kincardine town,
      The Firth of Forth
    Still down to the railroad bridge,
      Arthur's seat;
& in the shadows that we count
    Along the valley ridge
    A clarity that cuts & keeps.

There's still that evening eight years on:
    Your voice was time itself.
      We lay
      Stations
    On the Bel rock shelf
    & passed the longest day,
I saw the Pict in you & me,
The governance of love's slow, leeward sense
From the valley ridge to the silvered sea.
Now winter is the conscience lies between us
    Nothing but the past upon us
    All the clocks turned back.

Smogline

This earth is used to thirst & the stoic rocks
have lain here long expressionless;
even the olive trees grow & do not grow
with a perennial stature:
something of the Phoenician will survives
in the raw definite colorations of the land,
the resoluteness, the firm edge of the place

But the sea is invisible now most days,
the clearer climes of Mount Lebanon recede
as though one looked through glass
upon an eighteenth-century Japanese watercolour
& the confabulating haze, not yet an illness,
lingers on the stomach
adrenalizing vaguely as it sours.

Song: In Double Time

'Tis the Prophet's Birthday
& excepting the unfortunate ones
Doomed to keep
                consecrate the home
Peace to all, a
Men. 'Tis the Prophet's Birthday &
So rest the Children of Allah
                peace be upon him

Unless they be labourers & dig
The earth, rattle
The old bones & ring
Their ancient iron on the rock;

Unless their bodies sinuously sing
& percussively, an hymn:
The hand is slow that marks the hour of work
God knows, & full in praise of Him.

Each season
With a necessary knowing
Has its way of remembering:

The sky is swathed in plum-bands
Maybe, as broad night depends
Or the reason

For our mysterious illness
Comes down to one engaging face
In a dark & lonely place,

Brilliance or its lack,
The blinded thrash
To get the water from off our back.

But brilliance fails:
This light has not the knack
Of foraging always for our tales

Though it may be that loneliness
Should always press
That there must always be the threat

Of growing less & less.
Memory is fickle,
Does not always realize

It has stopped raining
That it hasn't rained for hours.

Strays

I

The auspica are dumb,
Give cry: the palsy comes
Like never of yore
The hailest go in fear

Like unto Cassandra
Discovered in the skein;
Loxias' regalia
Squaring up to the squad:

Many dark words of god.

The prone canticle
Of sapience is cut
Down to the cuticle,
The hot seam of the quick:

Dark words
& the blood comes thick.

II

I imagined my life in your weird womb,
America, in the future itself
& dreaming on its images: meanwhile
I hear the alarm clock on your bedside shelf
warning another prisoner has escaped.

I have washed my face with salt water
each morning since we met: I can't wake up
except this dull feeling, Dear Officer,
that you had my dream in your thuggish paws

but it *was* you I saw on the TV News
smiling with child & becoming the strait-talk.
Close, the world could see your honest moustache
bristle at the mention of injustice
& feel you were the kind of man to trust.

III

What now my love, wry hairveins being tapped,
fickle, & have I now more of your old sweet blood,
the coolsharp, than mine own that as it dripped
o during the first controlled singing, God
was it something? Red: ah but you forget

blood of your blood now reborn, capable.
I cannot wish you happiness from here:
the pith of life is not the beautiful
trip of March light at the bolted window
but hourly a motley assortment of pills.

Last time they strapped me to the bed
a recidivist to your fierce non-speech
who'd be the needled victim ever to your touch:
& when they probed my arm this morning nothing bled.

IV

Could I unhasp me from the drip & walk
out now, just I (say my body is my own
my patient wit comes clear), I'd soon have talk
& awkwardly be spoke with you: no white pill
-ow of valium, no delicious lack of focus

or other sundogs now. I would assail
the nightmare prince, reborn a harlequin
of frogs & *lyric lyric lyric* thrill
you straitly: a canticle of frogverse

born of storm to coax the quiet song
you used to mouth me when on Acheron
we were well-met: that old myth-ridden wrong
that fixed us unheroically abed
& loosed the phantom crooning in my head.

V

Frayed memento, the given garland of
a friend once worn around the wrist: I found
it lake-cast; how coloured so, vividly
in saffron, blue-yellow with the red wound
clear-in, I'll never know & that virgin weave

of puce! I wished that such a thing were mine
Dear Sea & all that broke it off was sand
& the salty strife of some certain she
eager & careless beyond all token,

regret an afterthought sad but glad to wait
morning's final shaking out of the clothes.
For moorish jealousy we'd wash & kiss,
friend, in this fantasy. We might then dream it,
hold it gone in its brightness vast as sea.

VI
Aquilegia

Said Columbina with the coalblack hair
I'm yes: *planting* rocks (my joke was secondhand
from Beckett who alone knows I'm sincere
in hopecraving in yespraying they *will* sprout
that never do): O the perplexity

the remoteness touching beauty:
she never had a chance to turn about
or laugh! Her coalfine hair will grow out &
still her name will be a mystery

her body always heaped, the gardener
& never the fantastic wished-for fruit.
I passed, thinking quietly to linger
there like rock & sup the water from her hand
fallen, Columbina, with the fine coalblack heavy hair.

VII

We have the lakeside park all to ourselves,
Winter is cold & beautiful & light,
The buoyant laughter of the wind-borne gulls
Circling & rioting incites
A feeling that we had supposed subdued,
But now we walk together once again
& remember that lightsomeness of mood
That comes around, it doubtlessly remains.

I recognize this feeling, know today
Will be filled in dreamy going-about,
Pretenses & fitful activity
To greet the world while hushed & devout
I bid you summon me & keep me by
Your side though all of errant space denies.

VIII
Passengers

For Irene

Over the city now the snow is ended
they come in with their puny morse: somewhere
bullet-points are stowed & talk resumes
its buoyant & disinteresting plea.
The passengers remember where they are.

I screw up, below, an earthling eye to see
slow progress between signals, a dying
along phone-line fixtures but in the palm
of my hand the miracle is averting:
as if the constellations further off
grew brighter

                or as though upon a wire
cast for fabulous fish we were depended
to feel the reflex of that other life
& dance in the present on its glancing lure.

On Battling Tides

From where Lake Michigan throws
thrashing its hills & hollows
to where the force is choked
irresistibly
on this beach-bed of rock
one warning comes:
                       that strength is spent
though we only play
though we delve & vent
we are cut & smoothed the same,
unceremoniously
cast in sand & loam;
                       bright gems
once, perhaps, & lustrous,
that had made love known.

Extricate

The assumption that love leads us
Toward happiness is false
It leads nowhere
Love is a road to leave off

In all we have striven most
Vainly to communicate in love
To be well understood we have
Only lost

For life will have its jokes
& its symbolism. My life is this
Trying to withstand the force
Of simplicity & chaos

How much has love to do with these

How it forebears to be understood

Lines (-Seoul-)

To the neighbor singing in the shower
In this absolutely silent world, in Slavic Russian,
I say to you you give my faintness heart, aid
The tenant of my decrepitude with a solid meal

The first of my internment in a vastness
Of most solitary confinement: a tiny cell
Within a tinier, within a tinier:

I had heard that humans live like this
As I hear the water from your body fall.
Do you know it peals upon the tiles?

For Mohammed

Like acorns in the cup
This morning, wanting sleep,
My eyes were overripe
For the longer mountain path
& for the risen breath
Of the lowing sea, beneath,
That blew upon Balamand,

So that I thought the still
Bright spent gun shells were
The vestiges of war,
& how the ruin-flower
Bloomed then upon Balamand
That otherwise was sparse & pale.

There flourished
As far as I could tell
A single blossom
On the whole expanse
A hardy mountain flower
Of violet veering into plum

& I plucked the flower
& I came down
& I lie awake now

Listening as the huntsmen's rounds
Toll nightly upon Balamand:

A coarse silence is upon wave & wind
& the flower is withered.

Seascape

Diana
of night & love

is here: her dark
her silver

the irrelevant universe
ever at her back

making & unmaking
in slow uncreation

her chaos
all intending form.

An art of perception
her motioning,

dedicated, carnal,
the utter knowing

of the sea,
the Earth's longing

for her womb.

The water must have
risen imperceptibly,
amplitudes of morse
disguising it & then
silence, & below
the sure freeze.

Four forgetful days
of slow discovery.
The creviced mass
tumesces, more
water is displaced
something dislodges
all our bulk in the end.

A slight animation
startles the fish,
buoyancy: slow
awful ascension.
A tiny thawing
& then more slowly

rapping through
the slender icefolds
among the rubbish
in the light of day,
the first nice day

for a walk by the river,
a body.

Portland Mute

I take the MAX south & east
skirting town. Nothing falls
from the SKY but the sound of RAIN
is imminent: the absent cheek
that ghosts my own.

A BLUEJAY winks upon the line.
A ROSEBUSH promulgates
humid perfume down
lanes. A sensitive MAPLE turns
inward in the dusk

& is radiant at night
teeming reds silver
-ing over & into black
(bewildering veil, this
privacy that invites all comers

because some flame-like miracle
has shook the inner form). I
among the stuff of the town
grasping mute as Idanthyrsus
for FIVE REAL WORDS.

---

* In the East the magic characters of the Chaldeans must have been hieroglyphics. In northern Asia, as we have seen above, Idanthyrsus king of the Scythians (quite late in their extremely long history, in which they had conquered even the Egyptians who boasted themselves the most ancient of all nations) used five real words to answer Darius the Great, who had declared war on him. These five were a frog, a mouse, a bird, a ploughshare, and a bow. The frog signified that he, Idanthyrsus, was born of the earth of Scythia, as frogs are born of the earth in summer rains, and so that he was a son of that land. The mouse signified that he, like a mouse, had made his home where he was born; that is, that he had established his nation there. The bird signified that in that place he had his auspices; that is, as we shall see, that he was subject to none but God. The ploughshare signified that he had reduced those lands to cultivation, and thus tamed and made them his own by force. And finally the bow signified that as supreme commander of the arms of Scythia he had the duty and might to defend her. This explanation, so natural and necessary, is to be set against the ridiculous ones worked out, according to St. Cyril, by the counsellors of Darius. Add to the interpretation of the Scythian hieroglyphics by Darius's counsellors the far-fetched, artificial and contorted interpretations by scholars of the Egyptian hieroglyphics, and it will be evident that in general the true and proper use made of hieroglyphics by the first peoples has hitherto not been understood. As for the Latins, Roman history has not left us without such a tradition; witness the mute heroic answer which Tarquinius Superbus sends to his son in Gabii, when in the presence of the messenger he cuts off the heads of poppies with the stick he has in his hands.

New Science 128/158

Valediction of the Years: 2013

For James Goddard

Her dates ran thus & thus: a minor life,
a one-volume-life in the performance
of menial sympathies—

& the shambles of her grace,
as of resilient lymph-nodes, of ampoules of death
zoning out, delivering, my beloved, you

who do not grasp but have always a prick
at your fingertips; firm enough to pass
for a grocery store or a tobacconist;

for you alone I sign this day:
that it is the evening of this new-year,
early, & the unchanging daguerreotype

of winter dusk, such as you must avoid to flourish
in your final dark & bookish shrug,
is already flaccid & full of clumsy intention.

Dawn's concubines conclude they shall be
hardly amused with your epitaph,
the unsatisfactory floor.

On the Level

I
At the Catedral Metropolitana de Oaxaca

So many altars: it's hard to be lonely
in this Church: but I cannot say if life means more
for all the old indefatigable colour:
I enter where, by the side door, no one sells balloons
or trinkets: the humble portal of the godly.

After many years all languages and the grave
of my mother seem one: an inarticulate
sorrow in birth & death. If I have been born again
this is the place: & if I have not been born at all

this too is the place. I cannot keep from tears
& rhyme, begun, becomes this sanctimonious
blether ah, mother, I would light a candle here
in this foreign place for you but that I have no fire
only selfishness, that wants, that scorns to want, of love.

II

Soft voice! I talk to you, a child
about our world of commerce
or rather we do not talk
but exchange the one excuse:

you excuse your open hand—& I
that I have no phrase of compassion for
your huge eyes & head
lilting like a sunflower tonight or
an English Rose—

We tourists are dying out:
to break the spell of your poor,
beauteous world we must exchange our glances,
forgetting the leaves about us whirled
uproariously by the wind,
the incalculable invasion of the true.

I am lost like so many drops of rain
in the night, like the freshened air
by this fountain in the rain
in the volcanic night:
& the name of the night is language.

III
To His Spaniel

Rest, boy, an' lick your wounds, God knows
Ye did naethin' tae deserve 'em.
Life's hard: an' yet a cannae think they're out tae harm
The likes o' us

We'll have tae toughen up
We too, mere creatures lost in the vast
Expanse o' night. Like spiders cast
Into the flashlight our shape

Hideously galls:
It disnae matter that we come
Feelingly nor whit for: tae them
We're strangers an' that is all:

Here, while I wipe yer weepin paw
An' keep the fire-ants from crawlin'.
It's no sae much ye are deservin'
O this maltreatment as that the law

Is cruel here
An' gives no quarter: if we clash
An' are beaten down why then the gash
On yer wee airm but shows character.

We cannae think oursel's nor great
Nor sma' but trial makes
More o' our frail stuff: an' for our aches
Comes strength tae compensate.

Rest therefore, ma wee man
I willnae disturb ye, sleepin, now
With ma writin' lamp, nor anyhow:
Goodnite so, here lie still till morn.

IV
Postcard to Ricardo Flores Magón from Teotitlán des Flores Magón

FOR ALBERT

Perhaps you never visited this town
The town to which they gave your name
But where no-one reads your books now
Or thinks a moment on your fame:
Your personable revolution
Leaves this trace, the same:

The first friend I knew was Captain of Police
& wore the facemask of the enemy
Your brothers; by day he drives the city ambulance
Or sits among his neighbors in the square.
His whole life he has lived just here
& I suspect his sympathies.

Of my uncouth stranger's tongue
The women are forgiving; that I had
Some sad lines of Neruda's well enough by heart
Seemed fair start
& I hope we will be well acquainted
All of us ere long.

Life seems slow, but a fervid affair
& I think I better understand
The simple wants of your characters:
The rich have leisure & the poor

Have their necessity: nothing changes
Though the land was gifted them:

Like choral the ancient mountains
Loom or linger in the night
Fugitive as the world you strived for,
For this land, for that same liberty
That they took from you
When they interred you dying in your name.

V
The Birds of San Felipe Del Agua & Others

I thought to live where the lime-blossoms are
& the blossom-breasted bird drops from the air,
To know that easy sibilance
The once,
Deep mountain-morning colour,
& therefore clomb into the foothills here.

But now the sun sets the hush is found
To vanish from the mountainside: what sound
But donkeys stricken in cacophony,
This nightly roostering for company,
The quickening incessant dogs, shot live round
Fired on the empty night, a brass band.

Our aching, wakeful bones so soon are starved
The marrow that your needful quietness—
Too needful, quiet bird,
Because our living symbol of repose
& but the livid voice is heard
Betimes—we can so ill afford.

VI
In Tuxtepec Jail

FOR SAM

The day is long & long
The birds are in their nightly remonstrance
With evening;

The crickets sing
As night begins its slothful dance
Across the ceiling
& long are quiet—

The shadows reveal all,
All that it is possible to say
In our two broken tongues
& they know it;

That silence seals
Finally
All accusations
& night is absolute.

Somehow every crashing of the lock
Comes shivering in shock
For someone else:

Some other's infant cries,
Some other woman's kiss & tender eyes.
Stone hearts own this bed of rock.

Ah but when she comes
Finally your wife & your newborn
In sad resuscitating joy: welcome!
The night is torn

That would smother us into submission.
As Time is the punisher of man
So is Love the enemy of Time
We declare,

Ineluctable, allied, ours;
Short, short her incandescent season
But no matter—
It is all we need for fitful sleep at least.

VII
Hanging Lights for Christmas

A sort of horrific translucency
attends them now, wishing shade
like the deep-delved worm;
coiled, alien,
colour of scorpion they lie
in the midday sun.

A few days more
& their bright constricting form
will be all about: set to dream
on the familiar boughs of the zocalo
their incessant cartoonish dream
like parti-coloured fireflies
on speed. So forlorn

an image—yet all the town is gathered
expectantly this afternoon;
There is no quiet, no place left to sit
& a gossiping like grasshoppers
upon on the air:

Another Christmas at the throat.
In the stultifying heat,
in the sunshine, numbing as the snows
that quieten the North this time of year
where you are
& Home is, I suppose,
still the gaudy pulse we know.

& as spectacular Time
prepares the yearly sacrifice,
she, wide-eyed as they wind these rope-lights round
each hanging branch in turn
& He, her father,
gleaming accomplice & partner
in the coming dance,
look on.

VIII
Birthday Letter

The leaves here shake
like gilt copper
though the weather
vane is stuck
pointing North

& the hardwood
& green hues of shade
so fascinate with depth
that a jungle
stillness attends all

my reveries:
your perilous bird-life, your sky
blue love,
your turmoil
without hypocrisy.

*

December—
your December—flooding south
now on your birthday
has lost its wrath
& chill power

to dismember:
Here on your birthday
is no branch bare,

no lawn is overblown,
none are weather-bound

at home in fading light,
no winter blindness comes
upon the eye or mind,
no long night goes by
without sound.

★

If the leaves here quake
with perennial summer
& their green-bronze, copper
-green shadows sing in the wake
say: *because the day.*

If evening comes briskly
there with gilt-edged clarity
& then the long shade
that lovers love
say still: *this day in token of.*

& as night wanes,
your birthday come & gone,
when, as like, I have not shown,
say, then, a vane points North
in distant Teotitlán

blowing warm to you
phrases of unweathered love
& all the gifts of the natural South
because it is your birthday,
because this raiment is your own.

Fairies

Half-stitch lurkers in a world newly woke
from intrigue into ideology,
Lowell's fairies knew no language, spoke
in glances peeking in
to that pensive realm: had he
in the severest conjugations
of his poet's soul not overlooked

something? The cipher sang refrain, a kink
in the smitten web-work of his book
before the inner eye began to look
away & the stalwart objector
revamped his conscientiousness
in the vaporish suffusions
of the wounded, wounding sonneteer.

His peevish fairies they just wandered out
of earshot, maybe, or else they were
traduced like his early Saints, a solecism
hardly nameable tho' all espoused. Their doctrinaire
ur-secret came to seem a bauble on the branch
of a sober half-century,
his sullen curiosity another.

If the truth is just a story that we tell ourselves
to continue on ourselves; if the words
do not matter & the restless obduracy

of the illusionist is all;
not what is spoken but the will
to speak, & to have spoken
what it is, what it comes to be?

Your exorable runes may fail
but your lazy fairies still
look out onto your poor, baffled page
wrought, like that tudor-ford,
a kind of bijou Boston prank
foisted on our post-modernity.
As if four doors could ever be preferred.

For Ariell

My eyes are dim, a boozy tiredness within
qualifies the lake's lustre: rain
scarcely perceptible, punctures the water
with innumerable silver points, I watch
its routine disturbance without thought

when, wink of colour on the brine,
arch & flash, a patterning of scales
before the lake explodes in local noise,
a twitch of fish in this, our own thin atmosphere,
unhooked, merely looking in.

I have never seen a flying fish;
I was however struck once in a verse
of Walcott's with their love of storm.
A forearm long or more, the first
(no fisherman, I never thought to measure)

but, waked in me, the watcher looked for more:
& they came on with curious regularity,
unobtrusive, familiar as the rain
that seems to summon them to our own pale zone,
bright blossoms of the living ocean.

Why do they yield to the calling of the rain
& huddle together, fins scratching at the air

I long to ask the fishermen, am shy
(they, too, are edged along the surface of a world
looking on): why should a fish wish to fly?

We talk in silences & sighs, as lovers
Wrapped in an immemorial dream of love;
Kiss upon pretended kiss we number,
Touchless meetings, now & evermore;

How fleet in love, how quick to remember
Its passages we are; through long absence,
Through immateriality we share
A stroke so light the flesh seems made of air.

The Law

Amiri Baraka is dead. I
never heard of him, alive.
I gave him an hour & a half this week
in three seminars. Fish in a barrel
they love the hook
& my shame & my pride met
for the first time, I think.

A Middle North

The water turned late August & the pulse
of sun on Tulaby is met with deliquescent green.
September disappoints—that is the rule
this far north—& the exorbitant patience
of the all-year fishermen
tends to the shore.

Early dusk, not much noticed now,
will settle with disinclination on the lake
within the hour. A protracted summer
seemed it would be consummated here
at this time in this spot; how
quaintly marginal

& circumspect we were. Eutrophic hearts
surface shivering & shagged in dulse;
our summer bearing has deserted us,
our love is lakish now. You idle in your work
& I separately revert
to an accustomed yearning:

Articulate & ravenous, we have been cruel
as much as blind; this leewarding
together here on Tulaby is not a kindlier
compulsion though it may be we cannot subdue
the stars or bare in compass with the poles
of the magnetic & the true.

The night we sped towards the casino
in our week-old rental car two lanes
were scarcely wide enough; a mad diversion,
agonic & apart, to peer into
the void of the road, the void of the slot machine
the heart.

It is late for poetry I know,
Too late; but how I want to show
I'm not incapable of love's glow:

You made me happy, once, & still
Knowing you touches with love's thrill;
I thought desire would last until

Our skin came loose about the bone
My love, or one of us was gone;
Not so; & yet we fumbled on

Becoming more & more estranged.
Before we knew it love was damaged,
A cold brutality emerged,

Indifferent, sullen, maltempered—
Yet we were as often close as birds
Companionably cooped-up. Words

Failed; we called this happiness,
Isolated in our own distress,
Knowing each other less & less.

We thought love a lonely barren thing
Yet dangled from its slender string;
Did we not know what that would bring?

www.ingramcontent.com/pod-product-compliance
Lightning Source LLC
LaVergne TN
LVHW041548070426
835507LV00011B/984